BE A BETTER SEN COORDINATOR

Tricia French

Other titles in this series

Be a better foundation stage/nursery teacher

Be a better nursery nurse

Be a better foundation stage coordinator

Be a better teaching assistant

Be a better literacy coordinator

Be a better gifted and talented coordinator

Be a better caretaker

Be a better primary ICT coordinator

Be a better primary supply teacher

BE A BETTER SEN COORDINATOR

by Tricia French

TEACH BOOKS

A division of MA Education Ltd

Teach Books Division, MA Education Ltd, St Jude's Church, Dulwich Road, London SE24 0PB

British Library Cataloguing-in-Publication Data
A catalogue record is available for this book

ISBN-10: 1 85642 354 9   ISBN-13: 978 1 85642 354 0

Printed in the UK by Athenaeum Press Ltd, Dukesway, Team Valley, Gateshead, NE11 0PZ

CONTENTS

In this book the use of he, him or his is gender neutral and is intended to include both sexes.

BOOK DEDICATION

I dedicate this book to Tony, Ross and Kate my fantastic supportive family and to my big sis, Jill Rennie. Finally, to all the children, parents, staff and Governors at Waycroft Primary School who have been hugely inspirational in the writing of this book.

INTRODUCTION

This book is written by someone who chose to be a SENCo; it wasn't dumped on my doorstep because no one else wanted it. Consequently, I have written it because I want to help others who may not be as interested in these children's needs. I have a genuine interest in supporting children with Special Needs in a mainstream primary school and a desire to ensure they have the best possible chance to succeed in mainstream. The book will hopefully provide you with a starting point for your own individual school and raise some questions for you to ponder, as well as some answers which you can easily tailor to your school.

I hope you find it useful. All things have been trialled and the ones that didn't work I left out. (Is there a 'You've been framed' for SENCos?) Enjoy...

WHAT DOES AN EFFECTIVE SENCO DO?

THE ROLE OF THE SENCO

Are you the sort of person who loves a challenge, an all-encompassing, time-consuming role? Then you are the right sort of person to be a SENCo. Did you apply for the job or has it been forced upon you? Whatever your situation, this is the challenge of a lifetime and can be the most rewarding job you will ever do.

You need to have patience and the ability to communicate with a multitude of professionals, especially by e-mail or by phone. Can you rub your head and pat your tummy at the same time? You will be able to achieve this feat after completing a year in the SENCo role.

Are you able to support children, parents, teachers, TAs, headteachers, school administrators, governors, health professionals, social services and LEA officials, all at the same time, while remaining cheerful? Well, the cheerful bit sometimes gets lost on the way, but it is essential for your well-being.

Can you file paperwork expertly and consistently? Can you find paperwork that you have put somewhere very safe because you knew that you would need it very soon? Can you find other people's paperwork which has been misplaced? If you can answer 'yes' to all these, then you are the person for this role.

Do you prioritise your day but remain flexible enough to change at a moment's notice due to a child "kicking off" and needing your immediate attention? Can you think on your feet to distract a child into doing what you want him to do? Do you remain calm in the most adverse of situations? If so, then you are the right person for this role.

Good listening is an essential part of the role. You need to listen to all viewpoints made and be able to clarify them; to instruct a way forward and lead others to follow you. An ability to inspire and lead other professionals in the school, despite the many objections people will challenge you with, is essential.

Always willing to learn something new, from both adults and children? Then every day is a new learning opportunity to work through. Building new friendships along the way provides a network of support for the SENCo from people who understand the role and the vast multitude of tasks it involves. It can be a very isolated position, as generally each school only has one SENCo. Consequently you need the hide of a rhino and the ability to follow through the courage of your convictions.

If you can answer 'yes' to all of these questions, then the job will be a doddle. If you can answer 'yes' to some of them, then you are well on the way to becoming an effective SENCo. If you can't answer 'yes' to any of the above, ask yourself if you are in the right job, as these are all essential attributes of a teacher.

Always remember that you have the power to improve the life of a youngster. You are the key which can unlock a child's world in order for him to achieve his full potential. You will make a difference. Even though you may need a magnifying glass to find the achievement, it will be there.

SONG OF THE SENCO

I will not lose any paperwork
I will not lose my temper with parents who don't care
I will not lose my temper with professionals who seem not to care
I will not lose my temper with children who appear not to care
I will not lose my sense of humour
I will not ignore the needs of the staff
I will not cry in public
I will not carry too much paperwork around and hurt my back
I will not show that I don't like the person I am talking to
I will not allow myself to be upset when decisions don't go my way
I will not give up on any child
I will not stop trying to find new ways to support children
I will not show that I don't understand until I need to
I will not lose my patience with anyone
I will not accept that there is no achievement
I will not accept that every target has to be measurable by numbers
I will not accept that no more can be done
I can make the difference, for I am THE SENCo!

CHAPTER 1

WORKING WITH CHILDREN

This is the best part of the job. This reminds you why you spend hours and hours completing paperwork in order to get the best possible support for the children. The work is varied beyond belief, but it can also be quite repetitive. It requires constant communication with all who work with the child, and this includes the parents. Parents can be left out of the communication loop and this can result in them becoming understandably anxious. This can happen when the support is mainly given within school, ie. before outside agency involvement. I have found that if I write a letter directly to the parents explaining my involvement, rather than relying on word of mouth, this is much more effective. I also ask class teachers to give parents the letters so that they can give them a bit of explanation, which is better than them receiving it cold and getting upset.

As SENCo you are in a very privileged position where you can really get to know a child well. Often you find out more about the child as they are either on their own with you or in a small group. This can help class teachers enormously, especially when the child has ESBD, as you can shed some light on the way that he thinks and consequently behaves. You need to audit the current needs of your school in order to establish where the area of need is greatest, through results analysis and consequently decide the best programme and year group in which to implement this.

SEN PROGRAMMES OF SUPPORT

There are plenty of SEN programmes of support. You only have to pick up any educational catalogue to see the wide and varied range available. Where do you start? The best advice I can give is to ask the Local Authority which ones they are currently using. This will mean that there is advice on tap as to how a given programme works and how to avoid the pitfalls. Look at the training courses in the Professional Development Handbook, as the courses often reflect which programmes are being run by the authority. Make use of the contacts made at the SENCo cluster. Go and visit other SENCos in their own schools and find out what they recommend. They, after all, are the ones at the chalk face, or is it now the interactive whiteboard face? You maybe required by your headteacher to support the work done within a child's classroom. If this is the case, then you will need to know the class' planning in advance so that you can plan appropriately for the children you will be working with. However you are expected to teach, make sure you keep in contact with class teachers so that they know what you are doing.

SEN PLANNING

Planning for SEN children takes two forms in our school. The medium term plans take the form of IEPs (Individual Education Plans). These must be written with the class teacher so that they know what your targets are and you know what other targets the child may have (see *Appendix 1*). Ideally there should be no more than four targets on any IEP. These should reflect the child's needs and be achievable. If the child does not achieve the targets, then the targets are too big and need to be broken down into smaller chunks. They should cover more than one area of the curriculum, ie. one English and one Maths. If the child has severe needs, then he may need more targets to cover the implementation of physiotherapy, speech and occupational therapy programmes.

From the IEP then I develop my own planning sheet (see *Appendix 2*) so that I can record what the child does directly in relation to what I am teaching. This is exactly in line with the way the rest of the school plans foundation subjects. It is important to provide some consistency across the school and not to be seen as something entirely separate. After all, these children are part of the mainstream school. As soon as I have taught a lesson, I plan for the next lesson. This means I can remember how the lesson went and where the child needs to go next. Sometimes it is the only record of what has taken place in the lesson. I found this quite a challenging way of working when I first taught SEN. I came from a classroom where writing and recording were vital in order to prove where the child was, to a situation where very little was recorded in a formal way. With a lot of the children I have taught, the emphasis has been on the process. I really struggled with this at first. I was very fortunate in having a headteacher who believed there was more to school life than recording everything in paper and pen format. Yes, there is a place for it but there are many other ways to achieve success (unless handwriting is the target). I try to link my planning to the National Curriculum where appropriate. Working on social skills does not necessarily cover this, although speaking and listening is an integral part of social skills and part of the national curriculum.

You have to trust the staff with whom you are working. A child does not respond in the same way in a classroom environment with 29 other children, as he can in a small group or one-to-one situation. Class teachers have tremendous pressures from Senior Management Teams and parents to make sure that the children in their care achieve their full potential. If the staff tell you that a child has not moved on at all since working with you, encourage them to come and watch a lesson in their PPA time perhaps and see how the child can perform in a small group situation. It may raise their expectations of the child, and consequently the child's achievement will improve. It may also provide them with effective ways of dealing with the child which they have forgotten. Alternatively, use the time usually spent teaching the child going into the classroom situation and supporting the child there. This will give both you and the teacher a better understanding of where the child is and what he is capable of achieving.

A sense of humour is vital for working with children who have complex needs. It can be very frustrating for all when they don't get it, but it is vital to have the ability to laugh at one's mistakes and realise that in the big scheme of things if you don't get it the first time it is not too big a deal. You need to be very observant in watching for the smallest independent achievement in children. Constantly ask "what can the child do?" It is all too easy to focus on what the child cannot do. In one of the schools I worked in, one of the children I taught had vandalised the toilets and I was duly called to inspect the child's inscription. My comment was "Well at least he's remembered the 'ck' at the end of the word". I don't think this was quite the reaction that was expected, but at least I found out something positive the child could achieve. Ask the questions "What is it the child does not understand?", "Is there a better way I can teach this?".

DIFFERENT APPROACHES

A multi-sensory approach will benefit all children. One that combines vision, sound and action will enhance any child's learning. Computers are incredible motivators for children. Specific programmes I have found successful are Wordshark, Numbershark and Clicker 5. The first two programmes consist of short activities in which you have chosen the particular area for the child to focus on. The activity is then followed by a game.

I find that boys, especially, respond really well and I dangle this carrot in order to achieve other things in the lesson before going on the computer. Clicker 5 is an audible word processor in its most basic form. It does have a huge potential to do many other things, but we haven't had time to master it yet. Basically, it is a writing support multimedia tool for children of all abilities and people with special needs. It has a talking word processor and clicker grids have a variety of uses such as talking books, multimedia presentations and labelling activities. It comes with high quality picture support so you can rapidly make useful and attractive teaching materials. The children really enjoy working on it, and in small groups I find it particularly useful for the children to practise their spellings while I listen to others reading. It allows them to be very independent and achieve good results.

MEASURING PROGRESS

Whatever programme you choose to work on with the children, it must demonstrate progress. It should show double the rate of expected progress of other children to be truly effective. The way to measure this progress must be a national standardised test that is recognised by the Local Authority. I have used the Vernon spelling test, NFER individual reading analysis, Gillham basic diagnostic maths test, BAS word recognition test, and Dyslexia Screener (an ICT Programme). You need to ensure that the first session you have with a child is spent assessing where he is and that the last session is spent re-assessing what he has achieved. This can be really irritating if the child is ill and you are unable to re-assess him until the next term, when he may have forgotten much of what he had achieved, so be warned! Find out which assessments your county recognises and make sure you have the up- to-date copies of them. Copies of certain tests are no longer validated and may need to be replaced. This may be initially costly, but is a necessary expense. You have to prove to everybody that what you are doing is making a difference, or alternatively that the child needs additional specialist support which the school cannot provide. Another test I regularly use (known as wave 3 assessments) is one which was provided by the county and which assesses the sounds of the alphabet a child knows, whether or not he can segment and blend and whether he can use word-building skills in order to read nonsense words. I have found this really useful as a diagnostic tool as it can form the basis of an individually planned programme for the child.

READING RECOVERY

One of the best reading and writing programmes I have come across is Reading Recovery. Our county has subscribed to this initiative, has about ten teachers fully qualified as Reading Recovery teachers and is training more. Yes, it can be very expensive but it does have good long-term results which are reflected in our Year 6 SAT results in English, where the majority of children have achieved Level 4 and above, with an occasional child getting Level 3. These children usually have other special needs in addition to literacy.

Reading Recovery is a daily delivered programme of half an hour intensive teacher-led work on reading and writing on a one-to-one basis. It is aimed at children aged between 5.9 and 6.3 Years. We aim mainly at Year 1, as this seems to be the most effective year to deliver it. It is labour-intensive and needs the headteacher's full backing as it takes up so much teacher time. The results, however, speak for themselves as the children usually achieve a 2c on the KS1 SATS and a level 4 at KS2 SATS in English. I have been teaching it for six years and have not found anything better for this age group.

Other SEN programmes I have used are Acceleread/Accelerwrite, a computer spelling programme and Phono-Graphix, an American programme which has helped older KS2 children to achieve some good results. Using the strategies of several programmes, I have also individualised a specific programme for a child where no one programme will achieve. Numicon is a very successful visual multi-sensory set of resources which we have used really effectively to support children with numeracy difficulties. A programme which was given to me by the Speech and Language Therapist and which has proved successful in improving the quality of children's writing is the Black Sheep Narrative Pack. (Black Sheep Narrative Pack by Helen Rippon, Black Sheep Press with Stockport PCT (2002) www.blacksheep-epress.com.) This consists of looking at elements of stories in isolation and then building up complete stories. The key to all these programmes is consistent intervention by someone who knows what to look for in the child's achievement and can move them on accordingly.

You may find that as a classroom-based SENCo there is no time for you to teach children with SEN and it is all down to Teaching Assistants (TAs) or outside agencies to implement programmes to help the children reach their full potential. Make sure you know exactly what is being taught and how. Try to observe at least one session in order to be informed, and suggest other ways in which a child can be supported. It can be very frustrating as you realise how much you know and how you would do things instinctively, rather than just sticking to the written planned programme. It is hard to monitor all these initiatives in a large school, but try to make effective use of PPA time so that you meet this need.

Handy Hints

- Communicate with the parents about their child and explain to them what you and others are going to teach him.
- Talk to other SENCos and find out what programmes they find effective in their schools.
- Find out from the county what programmes they are currently running to train SENCos and try to get on the courses
- Find out about the most effective ICT programmes available.
- Monitor programmes being taught in school by TAs and outside agencies.
- Assess children prior to going on the programmes and again three months after being on the programmes, to assess value for money and effectiveness for the individual child.
- Use the internet to find out about programmes of support available.

CHAPTER 2

KEEPING ON TOP OF YOUR SUBJECT AREA

Can you ever do this? With the government ministers we have had it has almost become an impossible task. It has become a game: spot the initiative that has remained a target for longer than one academic year and has been completed! I think the government suffers from 'initiativology'. Initiatives spread like a cancer and no one has the right answer which fits every school. I remember talking to a teacher from Crete who was amazed that, despite having a National Curriculum, we still spend hours tailoring it to each individual establishment. This does have a positive side, as the British culture is so broad and has so many

regional variations that it can play in our favour. However, there are times when we seem to reinvent the wheel just for the sake of it.

With anything new in SEN it is worth remembering that every member of staff has at least one subject area to develop. In some cases staff have several, and they all jockey for importance in the school's development. Aims have to be made explicit to staff so that they can see the purpose of changes that need to be made. There have to be realistic time constraints on any new initiatives, and staff will need gentle reminders to stay on course.

PROVIDING SUPPORT WHERE IT IS NEEDED

It is vitally important that you know what is going on in your school in order to establish what needs to be done. If you are fortunate enough to be able to go into other teachers' classes and observe how children with SEN are being taught, then this will give you an indication of how the subject is being taught as well as how the child is able to access the curriculum. I am often in and out of teachers' rooms as I withdraw children or support them within the classroom, and this means I get to see a lot more of what is actually happening. Remember, you will see a variety of teaching styles and you need to consciously think "The teacher has allowed me to work in his room. I am privileged". Some teachers can feel quite threatened by your presence, but over a period of time you become part of the furniture. Children are usually quite vocal in their opinions of how they are being taught, so it is worth listening to them, but try not to pick a time when the child with ESBD has just been reprimanded, or the opinion might be biased. Individual teachers' planning sheets also demonstrate how they meet the variety of needs in their classrooms.

It is worth monitoring planning to see how the curriculum is differentiated to meet the children's needs. The planning will indicate who perhaps needs some additional support in delivering the curriculum and who on the staff can support them. There is a lot of expertise within any school that can be utilised, prior to staff being sent on courses. It also means the person giving the advice has knowledge of the school and how systems work and often has experience of the children in question. This kind of support can be far more beneficial to a teacher than being sent to an outside agency which knows nothing about the circumstances in which he teaches.

THE DISABILITY DISCRIMINATION ACT

Under the Disability Discrimination Act 2005 and the SEN and Disability Act (SENDA) 2001, schools already have a duty not to treat disabled children 'less favourably' than non-disabled children and to make 'reasonable adjustments' to ensure they have access to the curriculum, information and the physical environment through their Access Plans.

The new Disability Discrimination Act 2005 strengthens the DDA 1995 and SENDA by broadening the definition of a disabled child or adult, and imposing on schools and nurseries a further duty to promote equality of opportunity for disabled children and adults.

From December 2006 schools and LAs will have a general duty:

- to eliminate unlawful discrimination against disabled children and adults;
- to eliminate harassment and bullying of disabled children and adults;
- to promote equality of opportunity for disabled children and adults;

- to take steps to take account of disabled children's and adults' impairments – even if this means treating them more favourably;
- to promote positive attitudes towards disabled children;
- to encourage the participation of disabled people in public life.

All schools and nurseries will need to develop a Disability Equality Scheme (DES) through consultation with key stakeholders. This needs to be in place by 3rd December 2007. Your LA should have additional information on this. For further information on the DDA visit www.opsi.gov.uk/acts/acts2005/20050013.htm.

SENCO'S ROLE AS LINE MANAGER

As part of my role I am line manager to the TAs. We are fortunate to have some of the most dedicated TAs who go the extra mile for the sake of the child. You need to be aware of each of the TAs' strengths so that you can make the most effective use of them. These are often the people who monitor the child's performance and consequently notice all the little changes in behaviour which can make all the difference. Give them feedback on their monitoring; this demonstrates how much their opinions are valued. We also implement a performance management cycle for the TAs. It involves them in being monitored while they are providing learning opportunities for the children in their care. It can show who may need further training, and this can often be done in-house by other TAs. It provides them with the opportunity to raise their achievements as well as their concerns.

KEEPING UP TO DATE

Monitoring will improve your knowledge of what is actually being taught in your school and how it is being taught. You need to be able to see how this links to the wider picture. It can be hard to keep up with the wider picture, as it is always changing. How do you do this? It is necessary to know of the county initiatives in SEN. Attending meetings with other SENCos (SENCo clusters) is one of the main ways I keep up to date. People are always willing to share the latest ideas. In cluster meetings an LEA officer from the SEN team is present as is an Educational Psychologist. This enables us to ask questions and receive information about the county's aims and achievements. It also provides us with time to share good practice with people who really know the role. We have six of these half-day clusters a year. In addition to this, a SENCo conference is held once a year, providing workshops for us to chose from as well as a keynote speaker. This again keeps you fresh in your outlook and enables you to meet new SENCos.

There is a yearly SEN conference held in London by NASEN (check out their website, www.nasen.org.uk). It is a showcase for all things involved in SEN. NASEN also hold workshops you can attend. It is really worth a visit, not necessarily every year, but definitely at least once. An alternative way of keeping updated is to buy into a publication that could keep you aware of any new developments. The Times Educational Supplement issues a monthly newsletter which lets you know the latest news on inclusion. NASEN also produces a wide range of informative documentation which is certainly worth looking at.

The internet is one of the most convenient ways of keeping abreast of latest developments. The government website www.teachernet.gov.uk has a multitude of resources just waiting to be used. It has a specialist SEN section which has a wonderful web address page with all the web addresses you could ever want. Another very useful website is the SENCo Forum at www.senforum.co.uk created by NASEN. This is almost a SENCo chat room. I found it so useful when I first became a SENCo. I could post my questions up without feeling stupid and be guaranteed replies the following day. I am always amazed at the times at which some of the e-mails are sent, for example 1 a.m. or 5 a.m., so I realise it is not just me who is awake at these times.

ROLE OF THE SEN GOVERNOR

Your school's SEN governor is one of the most important people on the governing body and you need to liaise closely with him. Hopefully, every governing body has a governor responsible for SEN. His brief is to keep the governing body informed of what is happening with SEN in the school. I tend to meet my SEN governor once every two new terms (or once every old term) in order to discuss the current children with SEN and the ways in which we address their needs. We also discuss ways in which we can lead the school forward. Part of the SEN governor's role is to be a member of the Inclusion Committee. This committee comprises the SENCo, the SEN governor, a TA who works with children who have SEN, the headteacher, a parent of a child with SEN and a physically-impaired adult who lives and works in our community. All schools should have an Inclusion Committee. We look at the access plans for the school, policies and procedures for SEN and Inclusion. Race Equality is also part of this committee's brief. We meet three times a year.

KEEPING RESOURCES UP TO DATE

Another area to keep abreast of is resources. It takes a long time to collate what resources you have already in school. Often they are in use, and not where you would expect them to be. I am somewhat surprised at how possessive some people can become over certain resources. However, once you gain people's trust that you are not just going to take 'their' resources away, you just need to know what the school has and everything can be shared.

When I took on the role of SENCo, I discovered that there were a lot of very old, tatty resources which were in desperate need of updating. Some resources were handmade, but needed to be remade using laminators rather than sticky backed plastic. Colours had also faded considerably. Some of the hardest-to-teach children were using the poorest of resources. If you are the headteacher as well as the SENCo, it must be very hard to justify spending money on a few children when there are so many other things that could be bought to be used by a greater number of children. However, SEN children are entitled to a broad and balanced curriculum, as are all children. There are so many resources available to choose from. Each has a fantastic description of what it is like. The people who write these descriptions were surely estate agents in a former life. What to chose? Audit the needs of the poorest- performing children with SEN. Compile a list of things that would seem to be suitable for these children and ask other SENCos or LEA officials if they know anything about them. From their advice, order some new resources and keep a list of what you have ordered so that this can be added to, as and when more are purchased.

The books I inherited were very old and contained uninteresting stories which would not inspire any reader to bother to find out what happens in the story. There is a vast number of exciting books available, as well as some true rubbish. Talk to the Literacy Co-ordinator, who often receives freebies of books for children with lower abilities. Boys are frequently the poorer readers as they would often prefer to be off playing football or out with their mates rather than reading (a very sweeping statement, I know). Trying to find suitable books for them is a challenge, but a lot of publishers now recognise this and are producing books to meet their needs about subjects that will really interest them. (There is a selection of suitable titles in the resources section at the end of this book.) Again, put yourself in the child's shoes: would it really inspire you to read a book with pages dog-eared and falling out?

TRACKING OVERALL RESULTS

Analyse end-of-year results with the Literacy and Numeracy co-ordinators. This will give you an overview of the whole school and will inform you about how the children are performing. The targets are highlighted according to whether the child has met, exceeded or not reached his targets. We analyse these every year and it has proved to be vital in establishing where the additional support should go. All the teachers' assessments are loaded into a data programme called SIMS. I am able to access this data and monitor the progress of children on the code of practice and those who may appear on it soon. SIMS can also generate a record of all the children on the code of practice and what their needs are. This has proved very useful to the head- teacher, who can access this information when discussing matters with parents.

Keeping abreast of all the information concerning SEN is a very tall order. I think you have to appreciate that you can only do your best and are willing to find more ways of accessing and presenting information … in time.

Handy Hints

- Find out all you can about SEN in your school.
- Talk to all people who work with children with SEN.
- Audit books and resources.
- Use the internet to find out more.
- Liaise with LEA officers and other SENCos to find out more.
- Purchase modern up-to-date resources.
- Liaise with the SEN Governor and Inclusion Committee.

CHAPTER 3

ACHIEVING TARGETS AND STRATEGY GOALS

I always remember teaching a child who had severe emotional problems. We held a bi-weekly meeting to set new targets with him and his parents. After a particularly difficult couple of weeks, the child shouted that he hated targets and would not attempt to achieve any more of them. I think this is how it can feel with so many outside pressures wanting their targets fulfilled by you and the children. Where do you start?

SEN AUDIT

The easiest place to start is to do an audit of SEN provision in school. It is the same for any subject area; you need to know where the establishment is in order to move it forward. One of the tools which I have found invaluable is the SEN self-evaluation form (*Appendix 3*), devised by John Ward who has kindly given me permission to use it in this book. There are five sections to this:

- the financial overview;
- achievement and standards;
- provision and access;
- teaching and learning;
- leadership and management.

This is not a five-minute job; it takes time to complete and you need to complete it with a member of the senior management team, preferably the headteacher. The bursar is essential to the completion of the financial overview, as he can often find the financial statements more quickly than the headteacher. They will need to go into the budget and find the amounts for each of the subject headings. It is vital that you know how the money is distributed for SEN in order that you can evaluate value for money on any strategies implemented. You will also need to ensure that statemented children receive their entitlement in order to fulfil the requirements of their statements.

You may be very surprised at the amount of money that comes into the school. Is it being used to the maximum effect? From the five subject headings I have produced a provision map (see *Appendix 4*). Using this, you need to ask questions about how much money the school puts into SEN teaching and whether it is value for money. This cannot be done in isolation, as the assessment manager will have summative data to back up your findings. We have put a lot of money into training TAs, as we have found that if people are well-trained they are much more effective in all that they do. It also values the major contributions these people make to the smooth running of the school.

I found it very informative to complete the achievement and standards sheet. It made me look at what was in place in the school and how well it was being used. I looked at the IEPs completed by staff and I was reassured that all staff knew how to write them and that they consisted of SMART (Specific, Measurable, Achievable, Realistic and Time-constrained) targets. Some needed to be tweaked, but generally the standard was good. It did identify an area that we have tried to address this year, involving the children more in evaluating the targets set.

I felt very confident about the third Provision and Access sheet. Each year I work with the assessment co-ordinator to look at the targets the children have been set and analyse the results. We concentrate on which children are not meeting their targets and what we can do to support them. I then work out my timetable of support matched to these children's needs. My timetable changes every two new terms (or every old one term). This exercise is vital. It provides you with an overview of all the children in the school and their performance. It also means that you are aware of the whole school targets for the end of Key Stage assessments and can support the staff in achieving them.

The Teaching and Learning sheet involves the Senior Management Team as they do many of the lesson observations. They are able to feedback their findings in order to fill this in accurately. It also involves talking to the children I teach, as well as those supported by TAs, and on the whole this is very positive. I am very reassured by the children's appreciation of what we do to help them.

The final sheet is, of course, perfect. Actually, I was really pleased with the results. The headteacher was very complimentary and altered the gradings I originally gave it. Again, I think you don't realise what you achieve as you have no bench mark. The head

teacher, who has been into other schools, realises the high standard to which we are working and can therefore see comparisons.

I found it quite hard to gauge the audit according to the new Ofsted gradings as I have not been part of a new Ofsted inspection, nor am I an Ofsted inspector. I found the headteacher really helpful in grading this because I erred on the side of caution, underestimating the grades. The headteacher's grades were much more accurate and had a better viewpoint.

From this audit I developed an Action Plan for SEN based on the area for development. I tried to find things that were achievable, in the first instance, within the year. Some things require massive investment, eg. regarding access requirements, so they need to be worked into the School Improvement Plan. In addition to this, targets have to be linked to Every Child Matters

(ECM), Change for Children Agenda (Children Act 2004).

The five outcomes of ECM are:

- be healthy;
- stay safe;
- enjoy and achieve;
- make a positive contribution;
- achieve economic well being.

Children and young people will have an entitlement to a core offer which comprises:

- high quality wraparound care;
- a varied menu of activities to extend and enrich learning;
- parenting support, including information sessions for parents and family learning;
- swift and easy referral to a wide range of specialist support services;

- providing wider community access to ICT, sports and arts facilities, including adult learning.

AFTER SCHOOL CLUBS

One of the things this has flagged up is the entitlement to after school clubs. In our school we have a great variety of after school clubs open to the children. We have managed to include all children in these clubs, but it has been difficult to find someone to support children with SEN after school hours. We did find a youngster from a local secondary school who supported one of our children in cricket club. This worked well and the parents were very supportive. Remember, however, that such helpers are just children and will need to be supervised by an appropriate adult. We are now looking into appointing a TA to work in a cluster of schools, attending after school clubs to support children with SEN.

TRAINING FOR PARENTS

We have always tried to include training for parents whenever we can. We have run two courses for parents on parenting, and these have resulted in parents attending further training to be TAs. We have also run informative evenings, one being on dyslexia and another on behaviour. We had about 40 parents attend each course in total. We presented the school's viewpoints and had outside speakers from the Local Authority to give the wider view. As the school hall is often let out to the community, it can be quite hard to book it to present these meetings. Just bear this in mind: the keep fit ladies can be quite scary when roused by asking them to either change their night or, worse still, miss a week.

SMART TARGETS AND GOALS

All these targets and goals, although they have a direct impact on the whole school community, do not necessarily impact on the individual child. Targets and goals for individual children with SEN are usually in the form of Individual Education Plans or Pastoral Support Plans. These are in addition to the classroom targets which every child has for the core subjects. You can see why some children can find it all too much. The targets have to be "SMART":

Specific

Measurable

Achievable

Realistic

Time-constrained

If the targets are not being achieved, then they do not meet these criteria and they need to be made smaller. The whole point is that the child achieves the targets and does not have the same ones all year. Sometimes this is hard for the staff to understand. They don't always look at the finer details of trying to unpack what exactly it is the child doesn't understand.

I found it really helpful to get a Local Authority official to discuss how to write an IEP with individual members of staff. This served to reinforce what I had already said and also picked up new members of staff. I try and support all new members of staff during their first term and help them to write IEPs and meet parents when discussing them. I use the approach, "Do you think it would sound better if we wrote……?" or "I know what you mean. Could we phrase it like this….?" This provides a very positive way of utilising the teachers' and TAs' ideas in the correct format.

PERFORMANCE MANAGEMENT

Another set of targets which every teacher has are those for performance management. I have found that it is easy to link these directly with what needs to be done in light of the self-evaluation form. This means that the targets remain achievable and you know what they are. They are relevant and will move on your professional development as well as making the necessary developments in the subject area.

ACCESS PLAN

It is now a legal requirement to have an access plan in place. This should not be written by you at all: it is the responsibility of the headteacher to write it. However, your advice will often be sought, as one of your priorities is to ensure adequate accessibility for all children. An example of an access plan is attached (see *Access to physical environment plan, Appendix 5*). We had to plan for three years, and chose this format so that it was easy to complete.

Handy Hints

- Complete the self-evaluation SEN form as your bench mark from which to start.
- Write an action plan for the year based on your findings. Make sure the targets are SMART.
- Link these targets with your performance management targets.
- Analyse children's results in order to ensure additional support is going to the children who need it most.
- Ensure a Physical Access plan is written by the headteacher and make sure you know what it is.
- Train staff and parents appropriately.
- Research what else could be done to ensure Every Child Matters criteria are being met.

CHAPTER 4

YOUR TEACHING ROOM

Are you lucky enough to have your own room? I'll bet the majority of you work in the thoroughfare of the corridor. You have consistent air conditioning as someone leaves the door constantly open, regardless of whether it is summer or winter. Your lessons always run smoothly, never interrupted by one class going to PE, then returning, then several classes going to and from assembly. No one ever interrupts your lessons with a quick question. You are never asked to keep an eye on a child who is making learning intolerable in the classroom. This is what makes you such a specialist teacher. Despite everything going on around you, the child still manages to learn and you still manage to teach.

If you are lucky enough to have your own room, this is the most important place, not only to you, but also to everybody else you come into contact with. It should be as welcoming as possible for all visitors, including the children. Others may think it needs to be a showcase of outstanding well-presented work. This is a tall order and puts stress on both you and the children you teach. How long does it take to complete work without spelling errors and neat correct handwriting? How many times does it need to be written out before there are no mistakes? I have an area in my room dedicated to pieces of work which children have done themselves at home and brought in. These are done on a variety of paper, but are there because the child wants you to have their work. They are so proud of the things brought in from home, especially when they go up on the wall. These pieces of work are certainly not the pristine finished products you might expect to see, but they are done with motivation and enthusiasm by children who often don't enjoy writing or drawing.

DISPLAYS

I have found the best displays have been ones I can use in my teaching, such as the vowels with associated pictures to create an image of the letters to help the child remember them. I use the children's work to supplement the printed work. They tend to remember more when they have done it themselves. It is always good to mount the work well, so that if their drawings are a bit wobbly they still see their work as highly valued when it is well-presented. It is fantastic to see children's reactions when they see their well-presented work up on the wall.

Three-dimensional displays of natural objects have been valued by the children. I have displayed wood, stones, fossils, a sheep's skull and leaves, among other things. I use a lot of different textures and patterns, and these have provided the basis for promoting speech and language as well as stimulus for story or descriptive writing. They can also encourage work on fine motor skills when being drawn or manipulated. This has also prompted the children into bringing things in themselves to display alongside the other objects.

There are certain things which we have up in every teaching room as a part of the school policy. One is the school's aims, written in child speak so that every child has the opportunity to acknowledge them (see *School aims, Appendix 6*).

Another is a standard poster of "What have you learned today?" This is quite useful as I have placed it right by the door and it serves as a reminder to me. When I leave the room with the children, I will discuss this while escorting them back to the classroom.

We are also expected to have emotional literate words displayed. I have found these especially useful when working on social skills with various groups. However, the words can be quite limiting, especially if the children are not able to read well enough to decode them, so I make good use of computer graphics of characters displaying these emotions. These are the emotional literate words appropriate for Y1/2.

happy	glad
sad	unhappy
cross	upset
scared	surprised
worried	angry
pleased	joyful
thrilled	down
miserable	excited
eager	bored
annoyed	hurt
afraid	amazed

Here are the words appropriate to Y3/4.

happy	glad
sad	unhappy
cross	upset
scared	surprised
worried	angry
pleased	joyful
thrilled	down
miserable	excited
eager	bored

annoyed	hurt
afraid	amazed
contented	delighted
depressed	tearful
enthusiastic	furious
pained	anxious

And these are the words most suitable for Y5/6.

happy	glad
sad	unhappy
cross	upset
scared	surprised
worried	angry
pleased	joyful
thrilled	down
miserable	excited
eager	bored
annoyed	hurt
afraid	amazed
contented	delighted
depressed	tearful
enthusiastic	furious
pained	anxious
elated	optimistic
depressed	despairing
restless	apathetic
weary	irritated

infuriated	livid
dismayed	astonished
agitated	nervous
bewildered	disorientated

Another poster we are expected to display is "Who is responsible?... I am", which has a mirror on it. I have put it roughly at eye-level so a child can calm down using the mirror if this appropriate for him, at this time.

Our school's crest is based on a ship, consequently our headteacher named every teaching room with the name of a well-known boat. My room has the identity of Noah's Ark; I wanted a boat which all ages of children would know. We have made a tapestry depicting Noah's Ark and all the children who have visited my room have made at least two animals. I also borrowed some large painted animals which the nursery children had made for their

own display of Noah's Ark. I had a display of the monkeys from 'The Twits' by Roald Dahl hanging from the ceiling. I felt that the whole room was warm, welcoming and bright. However, I had a visitor who specialised in working with children who had Emotional, Social and Behavioural Difficulties. He arrived in my room and commented on its energy. He later on described it as very busy and felt that it needed to be calmer and less vibrant for children with ESBD, especially if a child had been sent to me in order to calm down. I have reflected on his comments and hope that I have toned it down while not losing the warmth of the room.

One of the most important things the room should contain is a box of tissues. Parents, children, staff and I have all made very good use of these on numerous occasions.

ACCESSIBLE RESOURCES

An important aspect of teaching any children is that they can access the resources themselves. Due to the wide variety of needs in one school, it is necessary to have a huge bank of resources. Unlike any other room in the school, the children are likely to spend more than one year in this room, not necessarily consistently, but they still notice when things change. Never under-estimate the power of display or resources: children always notice. You need good, easy-to-reach bookshelves to hold all the books which try to capture the child's imagination. "Book of the week" recommended by an individual child is always good to inspire other readers. It's great if you write quotations about the book by the child, so that the child is expected to do little work other than the reading. Again, the child can see that his work and opinions are valued.

Large cupboards are useful to store various games and other resources necessary to fulfil your job. I currently have two major cupboards. One specialises in Maths resources and the other contains Literacy resources. I have tried to keep track of resources by generating a list of them with a brief description of their purpose. I need to update this and this is one job I am not so good at. In an ideal world, I should add to it as soon as I purchase new resources but nobody is perfect. These cupboards are so useful because they are accessible to all the TAs as well as the staff. The TAs do seem to be the main area of need as they often work with individual children.

A large filing cabinet is a must. Because some of the paperwork is so sensitive, it is essential to keep your filing cabinet locked. Each child who is on the Code of Practice has his own individual file. These are organised in year groups alphabetically. I always file children's paperwork from the front. This provides easy access to the latest paperwork and I find it works for me. Quick tip: as filing is one of the twenty-four tasks teachers no longer need to do, always tell the poor soul who you've asked to file the paperwork that you file from the front so that you don't have to do it all over again because they didn't know. You could even put a label to this effect on the front of the cabinet. Thus speaks the voice of experience. The children are expected to find their work files when they come into the room; these are placed within easy reach. This also means that, should you not be there, the child knows where his work is and can find it for someone else.

There are comprehension cards, available from different educational suppliers, which I put in bags and hang on hooks for easy access. As I have quite a few of these, only the ones I currently use are hung on the hooks.

I put levels of books in box files. These keep the books in their levels and keep them looking tidy so that the children can easily access them. I have two bookshelves, one totally dedicated to Reading Recovery levels and another one which has a variety of genres, including plays and poetry. The books are not just one scheme, they are a mixed-up variety. This is important as the layout of books changes, as does the structure of the text, and children need to experience a variety in their reading enjoyment.

I also have a box of books aimed at Years 5 and 6 for children who are struggling with their reading (some suggestions are given in the Resources section at the end of this book). These have been specifically purchased for these children and as I teach six of the poorest readers in these year groups three times a week, I can make sure they have easy access to them.

Parents frequently ask questions about their children's needs and I have found it necessary to know about a large number of conditions. I have gained information about a variety of needs from outside agencies such as Educational Psychologists, Occupational Therapists, and the Social and Communication Team. This amounts to a large quantity of paper work, so I have a smaller filing cabinet with the bottom drawer dedicated to it. Each time we receive some new information about a condition, I file it. It is surprising how often I have used this filing system. We also have a number of assessments which either I or one of the TAs go through with the children. I keep these in the top drawer of this filing cabinet, together with general information about teaching.

An area which looks very higgledy-piggledy is the place where I keep resources to implement an occupational therapy or physiotherapy programme. I have found that if I leave the resources in mainstream they are often missing or broken. I made a conscious decision to establish a collection of objects for children to use. It means that I know where they are, I can find them easily and replace them if necessary. These are things such as a round and long wobble board, skipping ropes, bats and balls, beanbags, lily pads for jumping on, accessible scissors, right- and left-handed, rulers with grab ridges for both KS1 and KS2 .

Handy Hints

- Even if you teach in a corridor, try to make it as welcoming as possible using displays as part of your teaching.
- Make sure everything is accessible to the child and that he knows where to find his things.
- Display children's work wherever possible to place value on it.
- Make use of three-dimensional displays as a basis for oral and language work.
- Be aware of school policies on display to ensure that your display conforms.
- Try to have a balance of calming displays as well as vibrant ones.
- Have good storage facilities and list the resources you have. It reminds you of what is there and others can find things if they need to.
- Have an accurate filing system which others can easily access if they need to.

A useful item in which to collect pens, pencils, felt tips and white boards is a handy open tool box. It can easily be lifted on and off the table, whether you are working with children or holding a meeting. It has everything in it needed when you're teaching a lesson. In the mainstream classes these boxes also hold the Literacy and Numeracy books for each group of children. It makes it so easy to move depending on what you are doing.

CHAPTER 5

WORKING WITH PARENTS, CARERS AND COLLEAGUES

Being a SENCo is one of the most isolated jobs in the school. There is no one else you can share the burden with because there is only one SENCo in the school. You have to be able to communicate with members of staff, teachers and TAs, outside agencies, children and parents, while maintaining a hold on everything, especially paperwork, and also teaching.

Where do you start? That is the first 60 million dollar question.

You need to accept that the job is never-ending and that everyone wants a piece of you. It doesn't matter how you are feeling or what is going on at home, people need you to act on their issues now. Tomorrow will be too late. I've never understood the work-life balance; surely it must be the *Life-Work balance.* But still you know that the job must get done.

Even if a child is one of the most difficult to teach, he usually has a parent who loves him and it is worth remembering that, even if it is through gritted teeth.

PARENTS AND CARERS

You need to get to know the children's parents well. They are the experts on their child so it is vital that you get their input. Parents also have a great deal more rights and power in order to get things done. The LEA will listen to them rather than you, before coming back to you for your advice. Often parents of SEN children have had very bad experiences of school themselves and do not like coming into school for any reason. Think about the room you hold any meetings in.

- Are the parents offered tea or coffee?
- Do they come into a meeting where all the professionals are already sitting? How would this make anyone feel, coming into a room full of people already sitting down?
- Do they know who everyone is and what their role is?
- Do they know what the agenda of the meeting is?
- Abbreviations are used all the time in education. Are you aware of which abbreviations are known to the parents and which are not?
- Do the parents have enough confidence to ask what an abbreviation or phrase means in this public situation?

These are all questions you need to think about, as you work closely with parents. Sometimes it is worth having a debrief of the meeting with the parent to make sure it is clear what the conclusions of the meeting were and clear up any other misunderstandings or questions they may have. These meetings can sometimes be very negative as they often focus on what the child cannot do; it is worth forewarning parents of this, but also during the meeting make sure that you highlight the strengths the child has. One parent asked the class teacher if there was anything about her child that was positive. Always remember that the job of parents is to stick up for their child. While you may find it hard to believe that there is a case for the defence, listen to what parents have to say.

A great amount of paperwork is involved with any child is great, let alone one with Special Needs. While the LEA tries to put all the advice in plain language, there is always a lot of it. Some parents can find this challenging to wade through. I have found the Supportive Parents' Network really helpful in providing free specialist advice for

our parents. They will also become involved if there is a discrepancy between the school and the parent. Their primary role is to support the parent and therefore they can appear abrupt, but they do know their stuff. I have found it useful to invite them in to talk to parents generally. Then I know who they are and they can learn a bit about the school, should the need arise for them to become involved.

The Code of Practice 2001 requires all Local Authorities to provide a Parent Partnership Service for parents. These are some of the things this service might do:

- Listen to parents' concerns.
- Help parents find appropriate information.
- Help parents to prepare for the meeting with the school or local authority.
- Help parents decide what questions they need to ask, understanding who does what, who makes what happen.
- Help parents write their contribution about their child's needs.

Contact with parents and carers

One of the main complaints many parents have is lack of communication with them. Always keep them informed. A quick phone call to let them know what is happening can often avoid any unpleasantness. It is worth logging these calls so that, should you need it, you have proof that you made the call. Try to keep all adults who work with the child informed of their welfare. This includes the School Meals Supervisory Assistants (SMSAs). These people are often left out of the loop and yet they spend an hour or more every day with the child. It is understandable if they respond to a child in their way rather than the way prescribed by the outside agencies or teachers if they haven't been told. The bigger the organisation, the harder the communication can be, so rather than just making any obvious changes, check everything else as well.

Parents can't always attend the meetings you arrange at the times you require. Allow at least two weeks' notice prior to a meeting. If you know that the parents work, try to table the meeting first thing in the morning or as late as is possible to accommodate this. Sometimes it is worth reminding the staff who don't have children how hard it may be to take time off work in order to attend meetings. Teachers can be so tunnel-visioned at times and are used to getting their own way. Allowing enough prior warning for meetings is not always possible, especially if a situation has reached crisis level. Often it is down to you to chair the meeting. Try to encourage the class teacher or headteacher to take the minutes, as it is really difficult to do both.

It can be hard to remain positive when parents can appear so uninterested. "It's always the same ones who come". I remember this being said after the last parents' evening. Keep on with it, as these parents will continue to spread the word to all about the good things the school is doing and it will rub off. We have held several information evenings for parents in recent years. The first one was based around dyslexia. Out of a school of approximately 450 children, twenty parents turned up for an evening talk. We had invited a specialist in dyslexia, who actually had dyslexia, to talk to parents. The lady in question had spent time in the school and got to know the school policies and procedures around this subject area. She valued what the school did and demonstrated how well the school did to support dyslexic children in accordance with her beliefs and experience. There were a number of dads who attended this meeting. One came to me and said "I wish this had been understood when I was growing up as I know I am dyslexic, but it wasn't recognised years ago. I was led to believe I was thick. At least my son stands a good chance of achieving more than I have with this support". This meant a great deal to me and it demonstrates the need to organise meetings like this.

We held another meeting which was focused around behaviour in light of the recent TV programmes of ill-behaved children. We held one in the afternoon and one in the evening, providing a crèche. This was slightly better-attended. Again, we invited an outside speaker to talk to the parents, as well as the head teacher and me, to put across the school's policies and procedures. We used PowerPoint presentations to demonstrate the class rules. Parents were appreciative of this. A comment made by one of the parents, during this afternoon presentation was that perhaps the parents who should be there never were! My point is: never give up. Keep chipping away at the mountain. Messages do get through eventually, but it may take longer than at first hoped.

WORKING WITH COLLEAGUES

None of the afore-mentioned parents' meetings could have taken place if it weren't for the fantastic teaching staff team of which I am fortunate to be a member. Every member of staff works incredibly hard to give the children the best possible education they are capable of providing. In some of the most difficult circumstances they remain cheerful and continue to look for answers to support some of the most difficult children. This is not always the case, but I think you have to view things positively. Teachers are very good moaners, they have all got degrees in it, but if you ask them to demonstrate something they are good at, it is a very tricky question. They seem to be very modest by nature.

One of the main concerns for any member of staff is lack of knowledge about an individual child or his condition. You are capable of alleviating this concern by providing a training programme. Establish whether there are any suitable courses available from the LEA prior to a child entering a teacher's class. Arrange a class swap so that the teacher can meet the child and raise any questions he may have with the child's current class teacher. Try to arrange a parents' meeting with the current and future class teachers in order to eliminate parental fears about how the new class teacher will deal with their child. During the first few days of the new term, make sure you ask how things are going. Is there anything else you can do so that the teacher doesn't feel abandoned?

Training does not only apply to members of staff with qualified teacher status it also applies to TAs. They will often work with the child more than the class teacher. They will be expected to know whether the child will be able to cope with the work going on in the classroom or whether the child should be withdrawn to do something else. They are very adaptable people but, again, they need training. One of the most effective methods of training we have found is to pair up with another school and do joint TA training. The SENCo of the other school and I met to discuss the training needs of our staff. We planned a programme to suit both schools' needs. This was part of my Action Plan for that year. We organised trainers to come into the school and split the cost between us. This meant that the two schools' staffs met and discussed their various roles and were trained in new initiatives. All staff said they found it really helpful to get different perspectives on what they thought was the same role in both schools. They also found the training very useful and have implemented it where possible.

Always keep the child's needs paramount in your dealings with all staff. There are occasions when you may come into confrontation with staff and you have to assert your knowledge in the best interests of the child. Hopefully, these occasions will be rare. I have found the coaching approach helpful. This is where you respond tentatively with suggestions about how the situation can improve, trying to get the staff to come to their own conclusions as to how to sort out the problem facing them. Be aware of how you talk to people and avoid listening to gossip. Never comment on hearsay. Be prepared to investigate things fully without jumping to conclusions.

When you arrange to see a member of staff, they soon come to realise that whatever you ask them to do will take time. If you are a class-based SENCo, you already know the amount of paperwork needed on each class will reach the top of Ben Nevis, even on the way to reaching the top of Mount Everest. Unfortunately a lot of SEN decisions made about children are based solely on paperwork, and this will always add to a teacher's workload. It's amazing how busy people can look when they see you coming. What I have tried to do is create monitoring forms using a tick and tally system. The attached form requires a date to be written next to whatever the child has done (see *ESBD Monitoring sheet, Appendix 7*).

With the class teacher we have listed the main disruptions the child causes and then listed what we do about them. It only took minutes to set up but is an effective way of measuring the frequency of the disruption a child may cause without being too onerous a task for the class teacher. A supply teacher could also use this. Any way that you can find to reduce the paperwork will be welcomed, but staff need to understand the importance of paperwork and realise that without it the child will get no additional support. The only way they know this is by you showing them the expectations.

Handy Hints

- Get to know the parents of children on the Code of Practice well.
- Understand the needs of the parents and do all you can to accommodate them.
- Establish good effective communication between parents and school.
- Provide training and information, giving workshops for parents.
- Appreciate the staff you work with and listen to their needs.
- Appropriately train all stakeholders in the school.
- Try to find less time consuming ways to complete the necessary paperwork.

CHAPTER 6

LOOKING AFTER YOURSELF

This sounds as though you don't know how to look after yourself. Of course you do, but sometimes you realise that the weak link in the process is you, because you are so over-worked and tired that you are not functioning at your best. However, you are the one person with the overall view of the child and you know the deadlines for paperwork. If you don't yet, you soon will, if you miss them. A lot of my initial learning process about paperwork was when I hadn't sent it to the LEA because I didn't know they wanted it.

One of the most important things you can do is remember that you are entitled to non-contact time in order to complete the paperwork, and the head should be sympathetic to that. Notice, I say 'should'. If you are the head as well as the SENCo, then you need time to achieve this. Ensure that you allocate yourself time during the week when you focus on SEN paperwork. A number of headteachers who are SENCos often do not have the time to attend the meetings they should, and often rely on minutes of meetings to keep them informed. This is hardly surprising, considering the amount of additional work they now have to do as part of the head teacher's role.

A frustrating element of the job is when people tell you things or give you things as you walk around the school, and expect you to remember everything they have told you. It is so difficult to later remember something you were told at 9. 00 am. Since then you have dealt with a child's outburst and met a parent. I always say to people "please remind me of what you say, as I don't always remember it". You are only human after all.

All jobs are highly-pressured, but this is perhaps the one that really has tremendous impact on others in the school. Your job relies on the effective communication between you and many members of staff. There are few jobs in the school which have such impact on the school community. Most of your work relies on other people's paperwork and on your deadlines being met. This not only involves other teaching colleagues, it also involves outside agencies working with the child. It can be so frustrating. If you get angry with people for not completing their part of the deal, you may find you spend a lot of time being angry, which really isn't good for your health. You need to have the backing of the Senior Management Team to encourage deadlines to be met. A sympathetic "yes I know how much paperwork you have to do" is often more effective than "where is it?". Even so, when you have been sympathetic several times I think the direct approach can be understood. An offer of help to complete it is also a useful tool to achieve your goal. A SENCo may not always appreciate how intimidating paperwork can be to a class teacher.

Use the network of SENCos to support you. I have found that when I don't know what to do next, then there is always someone who does. It is always a good idea to cultivate these friendships as no one understands the job unless they are doing it. It is worth keeping an address book with direct numbers of people you can ring and update it regularly. Likewise, update current e-mail addresses of relevant people. I am always amazed at how often people check their e-mail accounts and reply to them often more quickly than to phone messages.

Always try to remember that the child will benefit from what you are able to do. It is often easy to lose sight of the bigger picture, so teaching, talking and playing with children reminds you of why this job is so important. It is essential that you know the child you are talking about and this is hard to keep up to date with in a big school, but not impossible. You need to make effective use of your non-contact time to ensure you can monitor what is going on with these children in the school.

Another technique taught by an educational psychologist is to write any appointments in your diary in pencil. So many appointments were changed at the last minute and had to be re-scheduled, my diary looked a real mess. It was hard to work out what was happening on certain days as so much had been scribbled out. In addition to this, highlight certain appointments when they have been confirmed. This means you don't have to ring at the last minute to check whether or not the meeting is going ahead.

I have found it is always necessary to write down an action list. I cannot remember everything and keep a check on people I have rung and who haven't returned my calls. I tend to brainstorm everything I need to do in no particular order. I write short phrases, just enough to jog my memory. They look something like this:

- assess child
- ring EP re meeting
- photocopy notes
- write minutes up
- fax order
- meet Y3 CT
- ring S parents
- ring secondary school
- agenda for Inclusion Committee
- SEAL project
- SEN record check and cross-check
- file IEP
- find evidence for SEF

Some of these things are huge to complete, some are easy. The easy ones I just tick off when I have achieved them. It does give me a great sense of achievement when I see lots of ticks down my list. When things consist of several steps, like SEAL project, I then add more steps to my list. This is so that the headteacher and governors can track what is happening and see how results are achieved. This involves everybody, not just me stating what has to be done.

- write letter to team leaders about team meetings to take place;
- split pack into sections and distribute to teams to discuss;
- talk to team leaders and give them their deadlines;
- attend one team meeting to assess reception of pack;
- collate all PSHE planning;
- put onto school teacher network;
- feedback to LEA on implementation of resource.

I find this system really effective and it can be checked at a glance to see what has been done. A word from one who knows: don't leave all the bits of the list you really don't fancy doing till last, as you end up putting it off and putting it off until it appears as this huge insurmountable mountain which you can never climb. Do one of these jobs daily so that the mountain is climbed in stages.

One of the people you need on your side in the school is the administrator (it may be only one person or it may be more, depending on the size of your school). These people can really make your life easier or they can complicate it beyond belief. They can support you in word processing documents, taking phone calls, knowing other people at county to contact and providing you with excuses that you are busy if you really can't afford the time to meet certain individuals. They are able to filter the important phone calls to you, and know whose calls could really wait until you are free to deal with them.

At the beginning of the year make a list of all your Statements. You need to write in how many units the child gets, how this collates into the number of hours, who supports them and the month their annual review is due. I use this list frequently, as one of the things I am asked time and time again is how many units a child has and much support they get in the classroom.

Child's name	Number of units	Person supporting	Number of hours support	Date of annual review
Ross	77	Maes Knoll	10	July 06
Kate	144	Bott Illino	20	December 05

At the beginning of the year, I write in my diary, at the beginning of each month, the child's review needing to be done that month. This helps me plan the year out accordingly.

Another list I make for statemented children is that of the professionals who support them. I have a master list of professionals who visit the school and merely highlight the ones from whom each individual child receives support. This also helps when inviting professionals to the annual review. At a glance you can see who is to be invited. It also supports changeover to new class teachers and TAs.

We are no longer required to keep an SEN register. However, I keep an SEN record. Each class teacher receives a blank record to enter the child's name onto. We recently changed our layout to try and make it as user-friendly as possible (see *Appendix 2*). This paper record is then entered onto the computer by the admin staff, with my support. As I have already mentioned, in our school we use SIMS, and this means that all the data about each child has to be recorded on the data base for the LEA. It is therefore no extra work to print this off and keep a master copy. I have found this particularly useful when talking with class teachers and parents as well as with other professionals. You are able to see at a glance where the child is on the Code of Practice.

THINGS YOU CAN DO TO MAKE YOUR LIFE EASIER

- Eat lots of fruit as this does give you more energy.
- Drink at least a litre of water during the school day. You can be incredibly tired if you don't!
- Try to do as much work as you can at school so that when you get home you can relax and play schools with your own children…
- Drink in moderation if you want to. But bear in mind that if you drink too much, it does show.
- It is a life work balance and you can say 'no' to people. "Have you got a minute?" "Yes, but not this one!"
- Talk to other teachers. It can be a very lonely life as a SENCo

- Don't panic. Ask for extensions on deadlines if they are totally unrealistic. Other people can always say no, but are usually glad to accommodate you.
- Try to get regular exercise. You might need the discipline of going to the gym, or you could get a DVD and do aerobic exercises in the privacy of your own home.

Handy Hints

- Give yourself time to do the job.
- Make action lists which are in a book so you don't lose them.
- Tick off the jobs as you do them, so you can feel a sense of achievement.
- Be understanding of your colleagues' workload, but be forceful enough to do your job effectively.
- Use the support of SENCo networks to achieve your goals.
- Know the children on the Code of Practice.
- Write appointments in your diary in pencil.
- Gain support from the Senior Management Team.
- Support the Administrative Team. In turn, they will support you
- Make a list of children with statements, including number of units.
- Make a list of professionals who visit the school which you can highlight for each child.
- Keep an SEN record.
- Know that you can never finish the job. There will be always something else you can do, but know where to stop in order to have a life balance.

BIBLIOGRAPHY

USEFUL REFERENCES

Buttriss Jacquie, Callander Ann, *A-Z of Special Needs for every Teacher*, (file) London, Pfp Publishing Ltd., ISBN 1-874050-77-5

Cohen-Posey Kate, (1995) *How to handle bullies teasers and other meanies*, Virginia, Rainbow Books Inc. ISBN 1-56825-029-0

DfES (2001) *Special Educational Needs Code of Practice*, Nottinghamshire

DFES 0160-2006 Doc-EN *Implementing Disability Act* ISBN 1 84185 5294 PP3/D16/44434/1101/35

Kamen Teena (2003), *Teaching Assistants Handbook*, Abingdon, Hodder Arnold ISBN 0-340-81123-4

USEFUL RESOURCES

David Fulton Publishers (really good teacher books about all sorts of conditions/syndromes) www.fultonpublishers.co.uk

Incentive Plus (Social and emotional skills) www.incentiveplus.co.uk

Jenny Mosley and Positive Press (ESBD resources) www.circle-time.co.uk

Learning Resources (general resources)

NFER Nelson Educational Assessments www.nfer-nelson.co.uk

NFER Nelson Educational Assessments www.nfer-nelson.co.uk

SEMERC (ICT resources for SEN) www.OneStopEducation.co.uk

The Happy Puzzle Company (especially for dyslexics and dyspraxics) www.happypuzzle.co.uk

TTS Senco's selection (general resources) www.tts-shopping.com

Winslow (general resources) www.winslow-cat.com

SUCCESSFUL SEN BOOKS FOR CHILDREN TO READ

Boys Rule, series of books by Felice Arena and Phil Kettle, Rising Stars Macmillan Education (2004). Also *Girls Rock* by same publisher

Jelly and Bean Books by Marlene Greenwood, www.jellyand bean.co.uk. *The Extraordinary Files, Rising Star series*, Macmillan Education (2007)

The Xtreme world of Billy Kool, Rising Stars series Macmillan Education (2007)

Trackers, Oxford University Press (2006)

Wellington Square series, various authors, Nelson Publishers (1993), but recently updated

4U2Read.OK. Various authors, Barrington Stoke Publishers (2004)

USEFUL WEBSITES

www.bbc.co.uk

www.senforum.co.uk

www.nasen.org.uk

www.opsi.gov.uk/acts/acts2005/20050013.htm

www.teachernet.gov.uk

APPENDICES

INDIVIDUAL EDUCATION PLAN
PLAN NUMBER

School:

Name: Year Group: Date of Plan: Date for Reviewing this Plan:

CoP Stage: SA SAP S

What? What are the broad objectives for this child?	How will we know? SMART (Specific, Measurable, Achievable, Realistic Targets)	How? Strategies, Activities, Programmes	Who, When, How often? Roles and resources (Who will do what when and extra resources required)	Date achieved progress noted

Signed Parent ____________ Signed Child ____________ Signed Class Teacher ____________ Signed Support Teacher ____________

INDIVIDUAL EDUCATION PLAN – REVIEW
PLAN NUMBER

Name: **Age:** **Year Group:** **Date of Review:**

Parents comment	**Pupils comment**	**Teacher/support workers comment**
What went well? What needs doing?	What went well? What needs doing?	What went well? What needs doing?

New information/changes in circumstances:

____

____

Outcomes: Pupil no longer needs IEP Draw up new IEP
Move to School Action/School Action Plus/Request for statutory assessment

PLANNING MASTER

	Date	Year Group	Curriculum Area	PoS AT Levels	
Learning Objectives/Skills	Key questions/vocabulary	Teaching input	Differentiated activities	Resources	Plenary PDR Assessment CCL
Evaluation					

SEN SELF-EVALUATION: MANAGEMENT OF RESOURCES

School

The SENCO and Governor of SEN are notified of resources delegated for SEN within the school budget, at the earliest opportunity, against the following headings:

	£
Through Base level sen funding (15 for 15)	
Additional needs	
Statements	
SSENA consolidation	
Resource Bases	
Through standards fund	
BSNS allocation	
Income Total	

The school's spending on SEN provision is identified against the following	
	£
Providing a SENCO in line with the expectations of the code of practice (2001), the TTA standards (1998) and LEA guidelines to the role of the SENCO with regard to SENCO time and allowance: [Bristol SEN HANDBOOK]	
Providing pastoral and Management time in addition to that of the SENCO	
Providing training in SEN to ensure that staff expertise reflects the TTA standards	
Providing staff (teaching, teaching assistant and administrative) and resources (learning, ICT and other) to meet the requirements of statements in addition to those provided by the LEA	
Providing staff (teaching, teaching assistant and administrative) and resources to meet the need for individual or small group provision and in class support for pupils at School Action Plan Plus as set out in IEPs/Provision maps	
Providing staff (teaching, teaching assistant and administrative) and resources to meet the need for individual or small group provision and in class support for pupils at School Action as set out in IEPs	
How any standards fund is deployed	
Resources - learning, ICT and other	
Providing additional staffing aimed at reducing class sizes in such a way as to benefit identified groups of pupils with SEN	
Expenditure total	

The Governor's report to parents, or from January 2006, the annual school Profile, should also identify how these resources are used.

SEN SELF-EVALUATION FRAMEWORK

Give a score between 1 and 5 for each statement according to the following criteria.

1. ***There is evidence that this aspect is working very well and contributes strongly to pupil standards.***
   ***Score linked to OFSTED grade** Outstanding*
2. ***There is evidence that this aspect is working well and contributes to standards.***
   ***Score linked to OFSTED grade** Good*
3. ***There is evidence that this aspect is satisfactory but would benefit form further improvements.***
   ***Score linked to OFSTED grade** Satisfactory*
4. ***This aspect does not work well nor contributes to raising standards.***
5. ***This aspect needs to develop urgently and substantially. It is a barrier to effective practice and a key area for improvement.***
   ***Score 4 and 5 are linked to OFSTED grade** Inadequate*

Achievement & Standards (including IEP and all Code of Practice procedures)	**SCORE**	**LOCATION AND NATURE OF EVIDENCE**	**PLANNED PRIORITIES FOR IMPROVEMENT. Tick as appropriate.**
a. Whole school assessment procedures are used as a tool for the early identification of pupils with SEN.			
b. The school uses a range of diagnostic tools and the expertise of outside agencies to identify and review the specific needs of pupils.			
c. Pupils with SEN have their progress reviewed in line with whole school assessment procedures. Pupils' additional needs and progress are reviewed at more frequent intervals, generally 2 -3 times a year and changes to provision made as required.			

d. On average, pupils withdrawn for Wave 3 Literacy support make double the normal rate of progress.			
e. There is no significant variation in the attendance rates of pupils on the SEN record compared to the rates for other groups of pupils.			
f. The record of pupils with SEN is regularly updated and distributed.			
g. IEPs are focused on the identified needs of the pupils and reflect that which is additional and different beyond the standard differentiation expected of class teachers.			
h. Documentation shows a logical sequence of IEP, review IEP etc.			
i. Annual reviews (for pupils with statements) are carried out in line with national and local guidance.			
j. Pupils and parents understand the purpose of the additional provision that is being made to meet identified needs.			
k. Pupils are encouraged to be actively involved in all aspects of their IEPs/annual reviews and their contributions are valued and recorded.			

SEN SELF-EVALUATION FRAMEWORK

Give a score between 1 and 5 for each statement according to the following criteria.

1. ***There is evidence that this aspect is working very well and contributes strongly to pupil standards.***
   Score linked to OFSTED grade Outstanding
2. ***There is evidence that this aspect is working well and contributes to standards.***
   Score linked to OFSTED grade Good
3. ***There is evidence that this aspect is satisfactory but would benefit form further improvements.***
   Score linked to OFSTED grade Satisfactory
4. ***This aspect does not work well nor contributes to raising standards.***
5. ***This aspect needs to develop urgently and substantially. It is a barrier to effective practice and a key area for improvement.***
   Score 4 and 5 are linked to OFSTED grade Inadequate

PROVISION AND ACCESS	**SCORE**	**LOCATION AND NATURE OF EVIDENCE**	**PLANNED PRIORITIES FOR IMPROVEMENT. Tick as appropriate.**
a. There are clear entry and exit criteria for additional and different support, either in class or on a withdrawal basis, and these are consistently applied.			
b. Unless disapplied, all pupils receive their full entitlement to a broad, balanced and differentiated curriculum.			
c. Provision is planned on the basis of an annual audit of the needs of the pupils.			

d. Pupils with Statements: provision addresses Section 3 of the Statement.			
e. Pupils at Early Years/School Action and Action Plus: provision addresses identified needs.			
f. The school has a range of appropriate interventions for literacy, language and numeracy and other specialist teaching resources, including ICT.			✓
g. All staff are aware of the nature and location of resources including ICT and these are accessible.			✓
h. There is an identified area within the school for use as a quiet/time out/low arousal space.			
i. There are effective systems in place for the transfer and induction of pupils.			
j. There is effective liaison with external agencies			
k. Pupils can access appropriate personal support.			

SEN SELF-EVALUATION FRAMEWORK

Give a score between 1 and 5 for each statement according to the following criteria.

1. ***There is evidence that this aspect is working very well and contributes strongly to pupil standards.***
   Score linked to OFSTED grade **Outstanding**
2. ***There is evidence that this aspect is working well and contributes to standards.***
   Score linked to OFSTED grade **Good**
3. ***There is evidence that this aspect is satisfactory but would benefit form further improvements.***
   Score linked to OFSTED grade **Satisfactory**
4. ***This aspect does not work well nor contributes to raising standards.***
5. ***This aspect needs to develop urgently and substantially. It is a barrier to effective practice and a key area for improvement.***
   Score 4 and 5 are linked to OFSTED grade **Inadequate**

TEACHING AND LEARNING	SCORE	LOCATION AND NATURE OF EVIDENCE	PLANNED PRIORITIES FOR IMPROVEMENT. Tick as appropriate.
a. Teachers' planning (and other evidence such as direct observation) shows that a range of strategies for differentiation is in use.			
b. Systems are in place to ensure the awareness among staff of the particular needs of pupils and an understanding of practical ways of meeting those needs in the classroom.			
c. Teachers' planning takes account of pupils' identified needs.			

d. The Learning Support team (teachers and TAs) is involved in curriculum planning.			
e. Systems are in place to monitor the quality of teaching.			
f. TAs are well briefed for all activities and work confidently in a range of styles in mainstream classrooms and/or intervention programmes.			
g. All staff have easy access to current IEPs for pupils they teach or support.			
h. Staff meetings and INSET regularly focus on SEN and inclusion. Local and national guidance is effectively disseminated.			
i. Pupils with SEN understand the targets set for them and feel involved in the learning process.			
j. Pupils show positive attitudes towards the provision made for them.			

SEN SELF-EVALUATION FRAMEWORK

Give a score between 1 and 5 for each statement according to the following criteria.

1. ***There is evidence that this aspect is working very well and contributes strongly to pupil standards.***
   Score linked to OFSTED grade **Outstanding**
2. ***There is evidence that this aspect is working well and contributes to standards.***
   Score linked to OFSTED grade **Good**
3. ***There is evidence that this aspect is satisfactory but would benefit form further improvements.***
   Score linked to OFSTED grade **Satisfactory**
4. ***This aspect does not work well nor contributes to raising standards.***
5. ***This aspect needs to develop urgently and substantially. It is a barrier to effective practice and a key area for improvement.***
   Score 4 and 5 are linked to OFSTED grade **Inadequate**

LEADERSHIP AND MANAGEMENT	SCORE	LOCATION AND NATURE OF EVIDENCE (OPTIONAL)	PLANNED PRIORITIES FOR IMPROVEMENT. Tick as appropriate.
a. SEN and the needs of underachieving groups are included in the School Improvement Plan.			
b. There is a development plan for SEN/Inclusion Learning Support and this is regularly reviewed as part of an internal evaluation cycle.			
c. The SENCo liaises with the Leadership Team and contributes to the decision making process, including financial, relating to SEN.			

d. The school pays due regard to the SEN Code of Practice: The SEN policy is legal, up-to-date and reflects the Code of Practice and also the inclusion requirements of the SEN and Disability Act			
e. The school has systems to monitor the effectiveness of provision. This should include the number and percentage of children who: • begin KS2 at Level 1 in English and achieve L3 by the end of KS2 • begin KS3 at L2 or below and make a one-level gain by the end of KS3.			
f. There is a systematic record and evaluation of the use of all SEN/Inclusion funding.			
g. There is an evaluative report of SEN provision and access planning in the annual school Profile sent to parents.			
h. There is positive feedback from parents and complaints are rare.			
i. There is a statement describing SEN provision and all provision for disabled pupils in the school prospectus.			
j. Support staff are well deployed to make teaching work more effectively.			
k. Pupils with SEN are able to participate fully in the life of the school.			
l. All pupils in year 9 and above have a Transition Plan in place that is reviewed annually.			

Devised by John Ward

PROVISION MAP

Year	Differentiated Curriculum provision	School Action and School Action Plus provision	Additional Provision made at School Action Plus
Nursery	2 Nursery Nurses		
Reception	TA Support am and some pm support	• PSP behaviour support programmes	• SEN TA support • OT support • PT support • SLT support • Senco support • EP Assessment
Year 1/2	TA support for: • Early Literacy Support • Group work within Literacy and Numeracy • Peer support and collaborative learning	• Reading Recovery SENCo • S.L.T. programme • SENCo Assessment • TA 1:1 teaching to targets • Numicon	• SEN TA support • COSI Team Input • BSNS LD Support work • EP planning/review • OT support • PT support • SLT support • VI support • COSI Team Input
Year 3/4	TA support for: • Group work within Literacy and Numeracy • Peer support and collaborative learning • ALS Terms 4-6	• S.L.T. programme • SENCo Assessment • TA 1:1 teaching to targets • Numicon • SENCo led social skills • SLT programme • PSP behaviour support programmes • Booster reading and spelling SENCO	• EP planning/review • OT support • PT support • SLT support • Acceleread/Accelerwrite • SEN TA support LD • EP Assessment

Year 5/6	• TA support for: Group work • Peer support and collaborative learning	• Phono-Graphix senco & TA • SENCo Assessment • TA 1:1 teaching to targets • Numicon • SENCo led social skills • SLT programme • PSP behaviour support programmes • SENCo support for Year 6 Literacy • Booster reading and spelling SENCO	• COSI Team Input • BSNS LD Support work • EP planning/review • OT support • PT support • SLT support • Acceleread/Accelerwrite • SEN TA support ESBD

Whole School Provision Planned for Current Academic Year

- Termly meetings with Inclusion Committee
- Whole school inset on Excellence and enjoyment
- Whole school inset on ICT
- Whole school inset on Speaking and Listening

Access to the Physical Environment

Priority order of targets	Strategy	Resource Implications	Links with SIP	Time Scale	Target Achievement Date
Make Year 2 door accessible for Physically impaired Child	Contact Sue Nolan and Steve Ashman	LEA	Ongoing improvement of school site and buildings	ASAP	August 2006
Make Year 1 door accessible for Physically impaired Child	Contact Sue Nolan and Steve Ashman	LEA	Ongoing improvement of school site and buildings	ASAP	August 2006
Assess needs of physically impaired child for KS2	Contact VI team and OT and PT to discuss needs and provide written reports to be submitted to county. Contact Sue N	LEA + ?	Ongoing improvement of school site and buildings	September 2006	August 2007
Create calm timeout space in dance studio	Research lighting/seating for an area in this space	£2000 ?	Ongoing improvement of school site and buildings	September 2006-July 2007	September 2007
Ensure adequate lighting in all children's work areas	Invite sensory impaired children's team in to advise	£1000 ?	Ongoing improvement of school site and buildings	September 2007-July 2008	September 2008
Hearing loop installed in main hall for use during productions by the children	Obtain 3 quotes and discuss with the school caretaker and Sites and Buildings Committee	?	Ongoing improvement of school site and buildings	September 2008-July 2009	September 2009

Access to the Curriculum					
Priority order of targets	**Strategy**	**Resource Implications**	**Links with SIP**	**Time Scale**	**Target Achievement Date**
Make all staff aware of Acceleread/Accerwrite and provide training for TAs	Training on Inset Day	Course	Raise standard in spelling	ASAP	May 2006
Training for staff receiving ASD children next academic year	Send on County course	£200		May 2006	July 2006
Share good practice in differentiation	Staff meeting, create a thought shower	Time		ASAP	September 2006
Children to become more aware of their own learning styles	Training for all the staff on learning styles Assess the most effective learning styles for the children	Trainer		January 2007	December 2007
Training for new TAs	LEA funded courses	£300	Ongoing training for all staff	Ongoing	Ongoing
Disability issues as part of PSHE Curriculum	Audit the PSHE curriculum Modify the curriculum to include these issues	£100		January 2007	September 2007
Develop ESBD Lunchtime/Timeout club	Assess which children's social skills need improving	Cost of TA one lunchtime a week Games for children to play		May 2007	September 2007

Priority order of targets	Strategy	Resource Implications	Links with SIP	Time Scale	Target Achievement Date
Make PE accessible to all	Research alternatives to the existing PE SOW	£500		September 2008	September 2009
Resource after school TA to support the inclusion of all children in after school clubs 3 evenings a week	Write to charitable organisations to secure funding to pay for a TA 3 evenings a week	School to match additional funding		September 2008	September 2009

Access to Information					
Priority order of targets	**Strategy**	**Resource Implications**	**Links with SIP**	**Time Scale**	**Target Achievement Date**
To find out from parents the format for newsletters they would find the most accessible	Amend the admissions sheet to include preferred format. Add to any newsletter "If you would like this information in a different format, for example Braille, audio tape,large print or computer disc,or in community languages, please let us know."			May 2006	June 2006
Establish the best medium for a physically/ visually impaired child to access the curriculum	Audit by VI teacher Implement recommendations	?		Ongoing	

Waycroft Primary School

Aims

At Waycroft Primary School we aim to:

- Enjoy learning and always try our best, we like it when others do well.
- Keep healthy and fit.
- Feel safe and happy.
- Follow the Golden Rules.
- Learn everyone is important and brings something special to our world.
- Care for people and the world around us.
- Have fun together learning new things.

ESBD MONITORING SHEET

What do you do?	Verbal warning	Moved child to sit on own	Child sent to other class	Child misses break time	Parents informed	Child excluded
What does the child do?						
Shouts out						
Throws things						
Pinches others						
Refuses to do what is asked						
Screws up work						
Scribbles on others work						
Leaves the room without permission						
Other						